The Letter Nn
At the Grocery Store

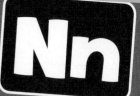

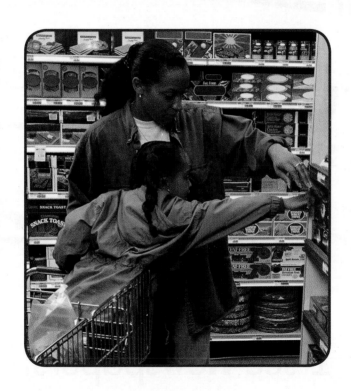

by Hollie J. Endres

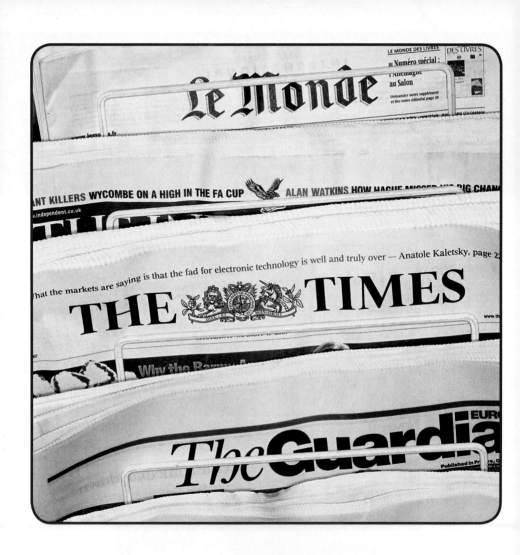

I see **n**ewspapers.

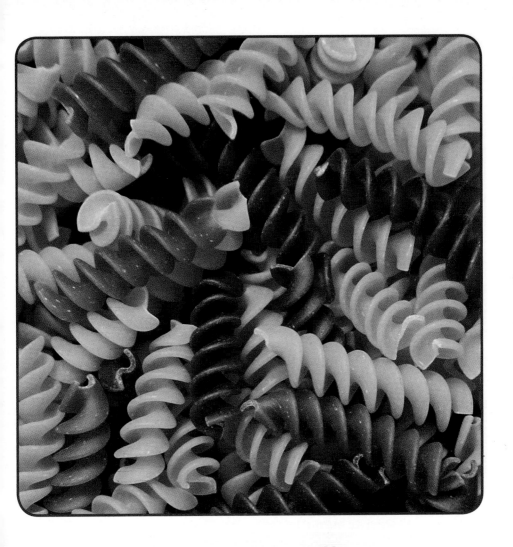

I have **n**oodles.

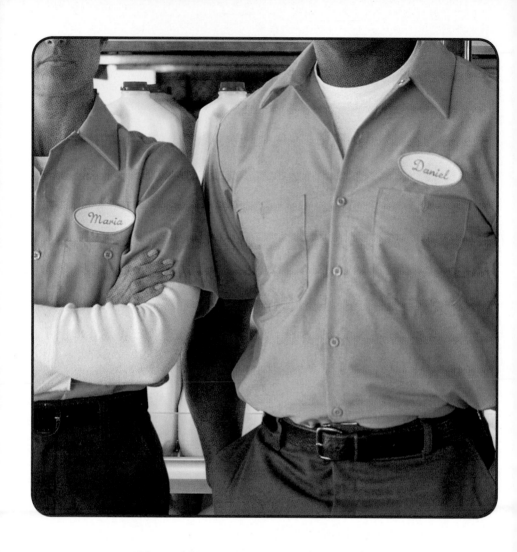

I see **n**ametags.

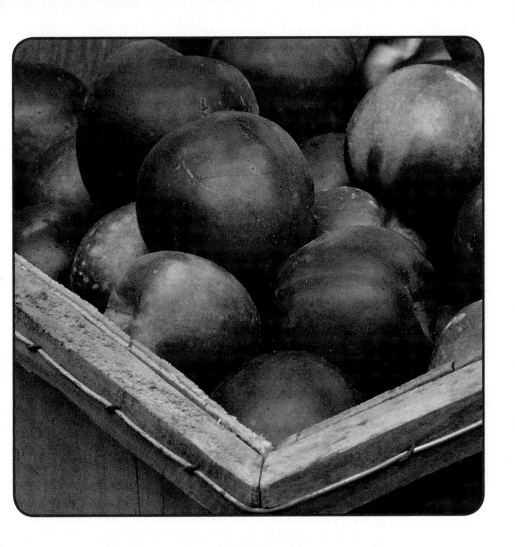

I have **n**ectarines.

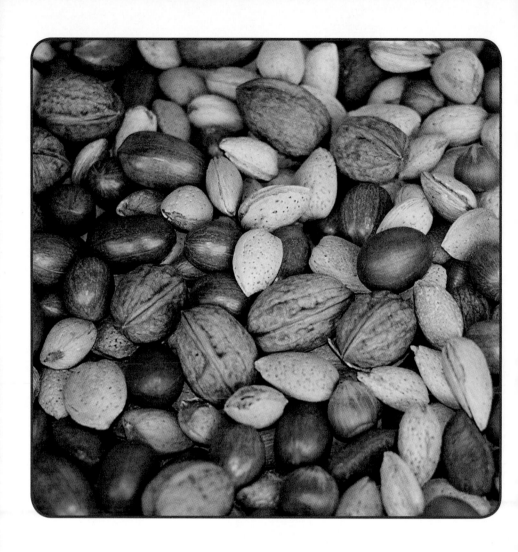

I see **n**uts.

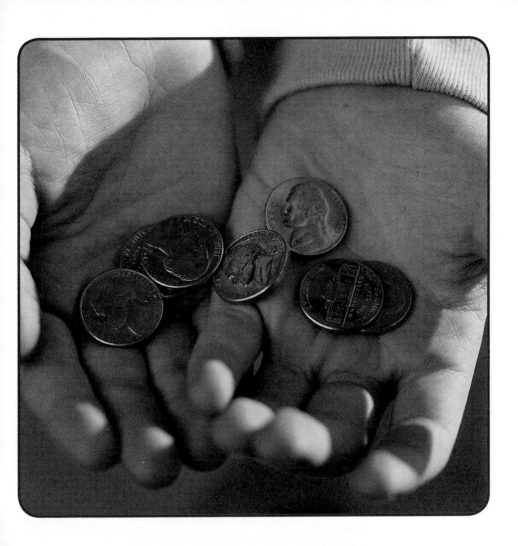

I have **n**ickels.

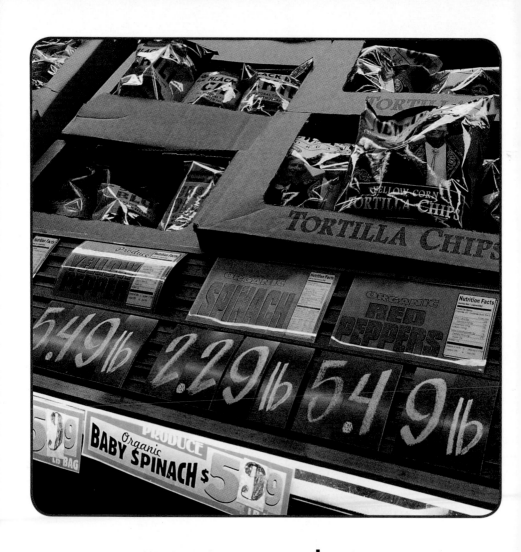

I see **n**umbers!